Meant to Be

MEANT
TO BE

Dave Nielsen

Winner of the Press 53 Award for Poetry

Press 53
Winston-Salem

Press 53, LLC
PO Box 30314
Winston-Salem, NC 27130

First Edition

Meant to Be
Winner of the Press 53 Award for Poetry

A TOM LOMBARDO POETRY SELECTION

Cover background,
"Gray and White Wall in Close-up Photography,"
by Mitchell Luo, acquired through Pexels

Library of Congress Control Number
2025932275

ISBN 978-1-950413-95-9

For William Shakespeare
1564-1616

Acknowledgments

The author thanks the editors of the publications where these poems first appeared.

2RiverView, 2024, "Momentary Musing on Earthquakes"

2RiverView, Spring 2021, "Sheepman"

2RiverView, Spring 2018, "Bullshit," "Run for It"

3rd Wednesday, Spring 2021, "It's You"

45th Parallel, Spring 2020, "After a Few Decades of Life"

Adelaide Literary Magazine, No. 21, 2019, "Big Time"

Aethlon: The Journal of Sports Literature, 2023, "Advice for My Friend Jared," "One Night Only"

Aethlon: The Journal of Sports Literature, 2022, "Growing Up"

Aethlon: The Journal of Sports Literature, 2019, "My Dad Will Go Down"

Aethlon: The Journal of Sports Literature, 2018, "Girls Rec Basketball" (as "For Rosie)

Aethlon: The Journal of Sports Literature, 2012/2013, "At the Thirty and Above League"

Apeiron Review, Spring 2020, "To My Daughter"

The Aurorean, Fall/Winter 2019-2020, "Ephraim Waffles," "Secret"

BYU Studies, Winter 2022, "Seeing"

Connotation Press, May 2017, "Dark Evening"

Connotation Press, July 2014, "Demonstration in the Study"

Folio, Spring 2017, "Heretic," "Sleep Tight"

Forge, Spring 2017, "How To"

Gravitas, 2019, "Walk"

Hash, December, 21, 2020, "Routine"

Havik, 2019, "Drums"

Hiram Poetry Review, Spring 2022, "Easy Does It," "Well Done"

Noctua Review, 2023, "Breakthrough"

Painted Bride Quarterly, Issue 90, "Home Office"

Plainsongs, Winter 2022, "High Dive"

Pine Hills Review, February 28, 2021, "Instructions"

Poetry East, Autumn 2017, "Lines About My Daughter"

Ramblr, June 2020, "Welcome to Your Position"

Redivider, 12.2, 2015, "Variety Show"

Rumble Fish, Fall/Winter 2021, "Epilogue"

South 85 Journal, Spring/Summer 2019, "The Way"

The South Carolina Review, Spring 2022, "How to Make a Hootenanny Pancake"

Southern Poetry Review, Spring 2021, "Motivational Speaker"

The Southern Review, Spring 2021, "Backyard Ball," "Strange Times"

The Southern Review, Summer 2017, "Failed Experiment," "Meant to Be"

Tampa Review, 63/64, 2022, "Prayer"

Tar River Poetry, 2023, "Years Later"

Contents

Secret

Sometimes late at night
after taking the garbage out,

I stop and take a piss
on the front lawn

and look at the stars
while I'm going,

at the lights still on
in the house,

and in the other houses
up and down the street.

If I've had a lot
to drink I can write

my name in the snow.

Meant to Be

I was conceived beneath the cherry blossoms
during the Carter admin. My father
was heavily into postwar Polish
poetry at the time, and my mother
had just spent several long, dark months lost in
The Cantos. Every other night throughout
the pregnancy a close-knit group of friends
would stop at the front door and sing lines of
ancient Chinese poetry to the quaint
notes of a lute that a neighbor boy
was always plucking. My grandmother threatened
to disown my mother if, boy or girl,
she didn't name me Rumi. Grandma said
the name could go either way. My grandfather
wanted Sharon, after Sharon Olds, which he
also claimed could go either way. She was
a relatively new poet back then
and he expected great things. My other
grandparents were dead. They had been murdered
walking to their car after a Ginsberg
reading. The deed was done by a group of
thespian street thugs who said a long work
by Aeschylus made them do it. Asked at
the funeral to regale the mourners,
my aunt could merely whisper a line or two:
Datta. Dayadhvam. Damyata.
Shantih shantih shantih
During my delivery my parents
hired an actor to read Charles Simic's
hit collection *Classic Ballroom Dances*.
The story goes my head began to crown
right between the poems "Prodigy" and
"Baby Pictures of Famous Dictators."

Demonstration in the Study

They were talking in hysterical voices
on the far side of the room:
"We want him to do a handstand
on one finger." What they were asking
was impossible. "We want him to recite
Augustine, in Mandarin, through his tears."
Truly what they wanted
was the impossible. "We want him
to fly around the room and land on the table
or something." What the French call
impossible. "We want a blood sacrifice
before he writes a single word."
Now it was just plain unreasonable.
"Okay, okay, we want him to write poetry
wearing a ski mask." At least
they were making it interesting.
"We want the mask to just float there
and for the words to appear without any hands."
Clever bastards.

Sleep Tight

After I bought the king-size mattress
and set it up in the bedroom
the kids came in, giddy as on Christmas morning
and began screaming and jumping on it.
They lay down
shoulder to shoulder to see how many
would fit. They did snow angels
with their arms and legs
and played Abominable Snowman
beneath the covers.
"Got yourself a new bed there,"
my father-in-law said, poking
his head in from the hallway.
He'd come over to see, a grim
look on his face, as though
the whole purpose and justification
for the bed was some sick fancy of mine
that involved his daughter.
The neighbors had to come over,
as though at an open house,
laying and bouncing and trying it out, so to speak,
winking at me, cracking
the most obscene jokes. By nightfall
the bed was full of strangers
from further down the street—a mass
of arms and legs that might have been
inspiration for the most grotesque
medieval statue. I could hardly turn
without having to make love to someone
I had never met before. Midnight a swirl
of softly heaving, sleeping humanity.
I stuck my hand through someone's armpit
and felt my wife's hand reaching back.
We locked fingers then, holding it
until my entire arm and shoulder fell asleep

and my hand went numb.
"I love you," I whispered
into the ear that was nearest me,
kissing it goodnight and feeling it twitch
beneath the brush of my whiskers.

Advice for My Friend Jared

No one takes a charge in pickup games, ok?

In pickup, what we want are good, clean,
straight-up fouls, no flopping.

You won't get any foul shots here.
Just the ball back. No one cares about your stats.

But we're still watching to see if you'll play defense
and body up the fat guy even when he's got his shirt off.

Basically, you're playing hard but without trying to kill.
Just take a minute and think about that. Let

the old timer shoot it occasionally, and the skinny
dude who chucks it over his head

like he's swinging an ax. Everybody gets a chance.
Sooner or later someone's going to sprain an ankle,

or blow a knee out, and that will be the end
for that poor sap. Could be me, could be you.

Could be a heart attack. The point is,
always assume the worst—because in all honesty,

on this court, it can't get much worse.

Years Later

Hiking up the mountain
the fork in the trail can sometimes
be hard to see.
You walk right by it, completely unaware.
Later on, you're wondering
how in the world
you missed it.
Or is it still somewhere up ahead?
On the way down
it's obvious, of course,
impossible not to notice.
Don't be mad at yourself,
try to show some compassion.
You were content then—
You just had no idea
where you were going.

Breakthrough

The roly poly
had only a moment
to enjoy the warm
dry hut of its body
rolled up tight
against the universe
before the worker's
boot squashed it
into oblivion.
But in that split
second before death,
in that infinitesimally
small fraction
of existence,
it remembered something.
Pretty remarkable
for a bug.

Motivational Speaker

I like my cozy cubicle, just
high enough I can't see over it,
though I can hear whisperings
of my coworkers, like ghosts.
Nor can anyone see me.
Through my window
I see into the nearby building,
the inside of another
person's cubicle.
Hello, brother. I see
a giant mug there for coffee.
Half empty or half full?

Welcome to Your Position

Don't work too hard, we'll start there.
Take as many pens and notebooks
as you like. Show up on time
and mostly stay until 5:00—
now and then a little bit later,
but really—try not to overexert
yourself. If you're asked to piss in a cup,
piss in the cup. In the meantime,
feel free to talk about the wife
and kids, especially when they're sick
or otherwise not well. Anxiety,
anger management, full-blown
cannibalism—you'd be surprised
how much we appreciate these issues.
Just don't put in for too many vacation days.
We'd prefer that you just sort of snuck out.
Be sure to dress up for the Cinco
de Mayo lunch every year.
When the time comes, and you know it will,
don't let the door hit you
in the ass on the way out.
Now let's check you for any hernias.
Turn your head and cough, please.

In the Aspens

If the tree's been dead a long time,
it goes over
rather easily, and for the next
maybe two seconds, ears peeled,
you just listen to it fall:
and the crash, the wonderful
splintering sound at the end,
is very satisfying—
like peeling off a scab,
that's all I know
to compare it to—
or if you've ever thrown a rock
through the window
of an old house
just to hear it shatter.
So that you push one tree
and listen to it go;
then another tree,
and listen to that one too.
All these years,
I don't know how many trees
we've tipped over.
But so far
we haven't run out.

After a Few Decades of Life

Today I stepped in a puddle of slush
and got my sock wet.
Then I bent over and accidentally dropped my glove

in the slush and got that wet too.
Then I slipped and got my whole leg wet.
"Son of a bitch!" I exclaimed,

before getting on all fours
and sticking my whole face in.

Big Time

Towards the end they stand and cheer

They clap their hands

They throw their hats in the air

They sit down

Now they are calling for hotdogs

They call and call

They begin screaming at the referee

Pointing and screaming

At the field empty as the sea

Someone bring them

A damn hot dog please!

For Rosie

This isn't one of those comp leagues
where kids have been playing since they were two
and parents pay for a coach, nice uniforms,
and a slick website. But you better believe
these six-graders want to win
as much as any five-star athlete
destined for the ACC,
even though they can't quite dribble—
not on a run. Sometimes two or three bounces
in a row. They slap at it with their palms,
that's the problem, and their shots
are all screwed up, too much
throwing or elbowing—
I don't know what.
I never take the Lord's name in vain,
but their passes, sweet Jesus, float like a balloon
or something drowning in water.
And yet even the smallest of them,
a girl who looks like she's seven,
can't believe I'm subbing her out.
She raises her arms, stares at me, as if
to say, "Coach—you're an idiot!"
For the next four minutes she's on the bench,
shaking her head, making me feel bad.
She wants a chance
at all the positions. Guard, sure,
but forward too. "Heck, put me in at center!"
She doesn't give a crap you played college.
She just wants to be out there—to touch the ball
once in a while
and play some really tough D.

Backyard Ball

What goes up must come down.
It's like a law of science or something.
And what comes down must go up—
it's like a law of trampolines.

And keep going up, so high
even a ten-year-old can dunk it,
not to mention his dad,
power forward in his mid-forties.

How does it feel soaring through the air,
legs wide, arms outstretched,
reaching for the rim?
How does it feel bulldozing your son

to the mat and dunking on his head—
screaming the savage victory cry
of a caveman—and throwing your shirt off
for good measure? Answer:

It feels good.

Growing Up

At night my dad told stories about the professional player
he used to admire who only dribbled with his right hand,

until a reporter asked, "How come you never dribble left?"
and he said, "Because no one stops me when I go right."

Dad would laugh, then look at me dead serious.
We both knew I'd never be that good.

So every day I shot 100 left-hand layups,
keeping track on a yellow piece of paper

I took with me to the gym. Now and then Dad would come too
and rebound, admonishing me to aim for the back of the rim,

get my elbow in, and to put some damn arch on my shot.
We'd end with a game of one-on-one,

me against the big man, all six foot seven of him,
mano a mano. The first time I beat him I was 12,

with a leaping-laner from the left side
that banked home soft for the win.

He'd been playing hard, and I knew it.
By the time I was 14, it was like taking candy from a baby.

There were games where I told myself
I was only going to touch the ball with my left hand

just to give him a chance, so that the game lasted
more than, say, three minutes. Twenty-one, win by four,

only I'd beat him by sixteen. All because he'd told me
that story about the dude who couldn't go left.

Momentary Musing on Earthquakes

When you imagine an earthquake,
you probably think of dishes rattling in the cupboard,
tiles falling from the ceiling,
roads opening up and swallowing cars whole—
bridges snapping,
buildings collapsing.

None of these is the real earthquake,
however, that you need to worry about.
The real earthquake

makes no noise,
sneaks up behind you—
exhales on your neck
colder than a blade
before entering in one ear

and exiting out the other,
more invisible than an electron.

Only your eye begins to twitch.
In a moment, your whole body is trembling.

Dark Evening

Late in the evening
in a brightly lit room,
and the windows
have all gone black,

it is impossible to see
what is out there,
only your reflection—
and the reflection

of a single bulb
shining brightly above you,
like a big idea.
And there in the mirror

behind you, ten hundred
thousand more of you—
your ten hundred thousand hands,
all of them

grasping for it.

The Way

The mountains east of my dad's hometown
used to feel pretty remote.
We never followed any trails
back then, just rode down

into one alpine bowl and back out again,
along narrow ridges
and across windswept flats,
through thick groves of whispering aspen.

My dad used to say that if we ever got lost
all we had to do
was give the horse some rein
and she'd know the way.

Once a week or so I talk to my dad on the phone.
We've come a great distance
since those rides.
I guess I want to say something

dramatic—about the horse inside me
or maybe the horse inside you.
What I want to say is maybe it's time
to test this theory.

Ephraim Waffles

The first part is easy: spread peanut butter
over the waffle—
then sprinkle grated orange
cheese over the top.

If you want to go all the way,
you could do Cheese Whiz.
Then the syrup,
which is a combination

of milk, sugar, butter,
and vanilla, all brought to a simmer.
I can't tell you the exact ratios.

To be honest,
Grandma Carol might not appreciate me
telling you this much.

Sheepman

My great-grandpa, Ralph William Poulson,
could shear and castrate a sheep
at the same time, holding the knife
between his teeth when he was using the shears,
looping the shears in his belt
when he was wielding the knife.
He could also castrate a horse,
or a bull—because basically
it was the same procedure.
He could grab a turkey by its neck
and pop it with a little flick,
hardly raising his arm.
People say he swore like nobody's business,
but I don't remember that.
When I came to visit
he liked to cut my hair.
I was only six, but I remember
he cut it so short
that once or twice it made me cry.
I thought I was bald.
He thought he was being sweet.
By his standards, he probably was.

My Dad Will Go Down

as one of the great hecklers of all-time.
He yelled at referees.

Not at the big sporting events,
mind you, not when he was

drunk, 70 rows up.
I mean Saturday morning

Super League, Junior Jazz,
sixth-grade ball over at

the middle school.
Each week introduced me

to a string of insults I'd
never heard before.

He wasn't a poet, but he
might have been:

rabbit ears, zebra, show some hair—
the way he mixed bullshit

with shit for brains
without ever sounding redundant.

Prayer

They say God likes fixing broken things.
They say he's particularly good
at plumbing, clearing drains,
stopping the little drips;
walking into Home Depot
and finding exactly what he needs
in under five minutes, a world record.
He knows how to use all kinds
of complicated machinery
without reading the instructions.
A whiz at cutting tile
and slipping it into position.
You need to replace an outlet?
God is your man, or God is your God,
if you know what I mean—
if you can get him to stop by.
You know how hard it is these days
to find someone.

How to Make a Hootenanny Pancake

Listen, I'm going to tell you
everything. Take a stick of butter
and put it in a casserole dish,
and put the casserole dish in the oven,
and turn it to 425 degrees
Fahrenheit. Take out one
of your wife's salad bowls
and stir up six eggs, a cup of flour,
and a cup of milk. Half a teaspoon
of salt. Once the butter's
melted, pour the egg mixture
into the dish and back into the oven
for about 20 minutes. Tell the kids
it's almost ready. Put the syrup
and powdered sugar on the table.
Look at how excited they are.
You might even give one of them
a ride to school. The little shits.

Long Drive

Another disadvantage to cell phones
is that nobody knows
any of the old car games anymore
when the window was the primary source
for entertainment.
The Alphabet Game, for example,
wherein all passengers must find
and call out each letter of the alphabet,
in order, selecting from the billboards
whizzing by; or Name the States,
which is, to go through the states
one at a time until someone in the family
gets stumped. And then, of course,
on the lonelier drives,
long nights on I-80,
after everyone in the car
has fallen asleep, the one I call
My God, My God,
Why Hast Thou Forsaken Me?—
peering ahead for the mile marker,
then starting over, peering ahead
for the next one.

High Dive

Up here
is closer to heaven,

and down there
under the water

is closer to the grave.
That brief second

while you're falling
must feel something

like death—
the butterfly

in your stomach,
the jolting clap

and sting
of your re-entry.

All the kids lined
up behind you watching—

one of them crying,
another

holding her breath.

Seeing

Grandpa Lewis is losing
his sight. None of us knows

what he can or can't see.
He's not like the blind

who develop exceptionally good hearing.
He's losing that too.

Sometimes he knows you're there,
and sometimes he doesn't.

Every morning he walks past our house.
I watch him from the window.

Now and then he looks over, as if
seeing for the first

or maybe last time
where his daughter lives.

Mostly he just stares straight ahead
and keeps trudging.

He knows sooner or later
he'll get there.

Easy Does It

My daughter likes to stay up late
and lie on the tramp with me,
trace the lines
that make Orion's arms and legs
with her finger,
then the Big Dipper
and the Little Dipper after that,
if we can see it.
I look for other combinations of stars.
I think they make a constellation,
but I don't know which.
Around ten I carry her into the house,
lay her down under the moon's soft
blanket coming in through the window,
trying my very best
not to wake her.
She was never asleep.

Lines About My Daughter

She could fall asleep
in a rainstorm
slumped atop my shoulders,
senseless as a sack of wheat,
as I trot a 5K
through the middle of downtown.
Yet promise her I'll read her a story
and she'll sit up waiting
like the wife of an old New England
fisherman, till I flop onto the bed next to her
and open a book;
scolding me to the finish
for skipping
this or that paragraph,
when she can't even read—
closing her eyes
when at last the story's complete;
asleep before the light is out.

Well Done

The only good poems you ever wrote
were the ones you gave up on.
You found them, years later,
in the cave where you kept them,
at the bottom of an ocean
inside your heart—not the worked over
hot dog batter that you tweaked
a thousand times, thinking you
were getting closer.
The only good thing you ever wrote
you got down without any thinking at all.
And now that you're old,
washed up and poor, the odds
are against you that something like
that could ever happen a second time.
The only great poem you ever wrote
is inside you still, though it might
never come out again. Just be happy
that it's there, and feel it sometimes
when you're outside and smell
the orchard, or hear the fruit
falling to the ground. It's right
there, forever. No one
can take it from you.

Uintas

That summer we built some good fires
up in the mountains
the kind I think you could see
from outer space
branches of dead aspen and dead pine
that we gathered with our hands
and snapped across our knees
into smaller pieces
sometimes jumped on with both feet
to crack and sometimes whole trunks
that we laid across the ring of rocks
and let the fire burn in two
fires so hot
we could have written an encyclopedia
on the colors of fire
the reds and the oranges and the violets
which was only the beginning
and in the early minutes after midnight
a glowing shimmering white
that you'd have to peer in at
through the top logs to see
how the eyes would just stay there
now that was a good fire
and in the morning the ash as soft
and light as anything
you've ever run your hand through
but only the top half-inch
because deeper than that would burn you
could cause you great pain
like I said that was a good fire
and lucky for us we had quite a few of them
that summer not to cook on or roast
or even stay warm by
just to stare into for a few hours
to listen and stare some more.

Drums

The maple trees
are sleeping.
The children breathe

quietly. The fall
breeze flows
down from the canyon.

When the Big
Dipper appears,
I long for

whatever is missing.
I don't know what it is.
Sometimes, I

can feel my heart
beating
inside my chest

above the sound
of a quieter,
more distant pounding.

Hungry

Dark night, outline of the peak.
Sometimes, from all the way down here,
you can catch a pinprick of light—
lonely hiker, lucky she's
got a flashlight. Hurry down,
something's brooding up there.
I don't know what it is,
but I can feel it.
In the morning, everything's changed.
The mountain's safe now.
Whatever it was
reaching with its gaping mouth
wide after us
is gone.

Failed Experiment

Better to be a big fish in a little pond,
so he moves into the country
to a town of a few people.
Little does he know they are all of them poets,
that the first has written a biography
of you-know-who,
and the second, the definitive analysis
of the most important one since,
and that they all write poems,
beautiful little lyrics
that they paint on their doors
and above their closets
and have tattooed across the buttocks—
painfully moving and intense—
so that he is, in reality, a very little fish
in an incredibly little pond,
more like plankton, really,
or plankter, to use the singular.

Heretic

Late at night
the letters slip from their words
one letter at a time
like tiny ships

following the stars
the sound of water
waves in the distance
to sail across the page of everything that has ever been written

to a new page where nothing at all
has been written
a new country where all letters are free
to be

their own word
to make whatever sounds
they wish
anything is possible

How To

Sometimes the instructions
for the most mundane task
can be poetic—
step-by-step guides for how to tie one's shoes
or boil water;

so too instructions for something
theretofore private,
rare,
or exotic:

dressing the dead, for instance, or dancing a rumba:
unstick the elbow;
now glue the lips.

Point the nose
as if staring into the future.
You can see
how these things might move you.

Run for It

Sometimes if I listen carefully
I can hear my daughter
arranging the furniture
in the dollhouse behind me

a chair scraping across the floor
a table pushed up against the wall
the little fake food
clicking against the plastic plates

my own wrist watch
ticking like a grandfather clock
and if the window is open
something bigger

a car
the wind yes
the mountain
like a great big animal

breathing through the screen

Bullshit

In my house the plates
have been known to wash themselves.

The clothes too,
piled in a heap on the couch,

hot after the dryer,
have, from time to time, risen up,

crossed, and folded themselves,
like some kind of resurrection.

You say the bathroom won't tidy itself,
but maybe it will.

Maybe it all happens
best when you aren't looking.

In the bedroom the god of this story
sleeps soundlessly

beneath a silver moon.

Comfort

At the end of your life
when the fat lady has finally sung,
big, fat, enormous, with incredible lungs,
and the tune is echoing in your brain,
what will you remember,
what will you look back on
with joy and longing?
The image of a child,
the smell of a room,
the sound of a friend's voice—
and what will be your final words
or word
after you've taken your final breath,
when there are only seconds
or perhaps one second,
after you can no longer blow out
the words even—
what will your final thought be?
Something less than profound,
don't put too much pressure on yourself,
it never works out
like it does in the movies—
only try to think of the breeze,
focus on it,
try to climb on board it
as you would a train.
A train, have faith,
that is going somewhere.

It's You

The dog knows it's you
before I do,

before I can see
or even hear you.

You park the car
out on the street,

you step onto the evening lawn.
All this in what seems to me

like total silence.
I am only a split second

behind the dog,
however,

for as soon as the dog stands
and looks at the door,

then I, too,
know

that it's you.

The Box

Just be patient, my friend.
Just be patient, my friend.
Just be patient, my friend.
Just be patient, my friend.
Just be patient, my friend.
Just be patient, my friend.
Just be patient, my friend.
Just be patient, my friend.
Just be patient, my friend.
Just be patient, my friend.
Just be patient, my friend.

Think outside the box.

Instructions

When you pass someone famous on the sidewalk
don't turn your head and cough.
When you pass a fancy car parked on the street
don't rub your finger along its hood.
When you walk past a hospital
don't try to peek through the windows
of the sick rooms.
When you're on the sidewalk and it begins to rain
don't look up.
When you see lightning
don't check your shoes to see how thick your soles are.
They're not thick enough!
When you hear a voice from heaven calling your name
don't answer. When you see someone
walk face-first into a streetlamp
don't laugh.

Routine

In the morning I pour myself
a plastic cup of A&W root beer.

It's too early for milk.
Then I go downstairs and try to listen

to the mouse running between
the floorboards.

Every now and then I think
I hear something.

I get really quiet
and try to crane my ears,

you know? Only it isn't the mouse.
After a few minutes I feel

a giant burp coming on—
almost like inspiration,

but not really.

Variety Show

Now that the ancient Chinese poems have all been translated
and the old ways paved over
and the sickos all cured
through the responsible use of electroshock therapy
now that the male has been proven
entirely unnecessary and superfluous
to the future of civilization
the cannibals all converted
and the politicians lined up in a garden
to have their photos taken
now that human suffering has been tested
to be nothing more than human suffering
and the moon utterly uninhabited

I wish to do a little dance
I wish to make a tapping sound all with my feet

Home Office

He sits down at his computer
and opens a folder

and discovers a folder
he'd forgotten about

and opens it
and discovers another folder

he doesn't recognize
and opens it

and now a folder
a sort of backup

he remembers creating
years ago

and opens it
and discovers a folder

so deep inside the computer,
he turns around

seeing himself
through the wrong end

of a telescope
and at last comes to a folder

The Very First Folder
and hesitates

his finger slipping
just enough

that all of the folders collapse
—so close

so close

What the Freak Are You Talking About, Man?

And what I've learned is
running uphill
gets easier

as long as you
keep
running.

At the Thirty and Above League

He hasn't played in at least a year,
and his shoes might be older than his daughter,
who sits on a bleacher reading a book,
indifferent to the miracle unfolding
on the court—her father,
no longer able to grab the rim,
or even touch his toes, yet tonight
he's been loosed into the pump and flow
of the game, with a shot that still looks mint.

Tonight his prime comes back to him
like a friend he hasn't seen
in maybe ten years—and though this defense
couldn't guard an x painted to the floor,
swishes are swishes no matter who
you're playing, and the four people in the stands
know it, except for his daughter, speed-reader,
whose page turning can't keep pace
with her old man's scoring.

She's missing "the greatest single-game performance"
the score keeper's ever seen—
counting the ones on TV, he says,
a sacrilegious claim that does nothing
to jinx what's happening: the fat subs
on the bench rocking back and forth,
nearly falling off their seats
after a deep three from the corner,
laughing curses so foul even she looks up—

Strange Times

These days something's different
on our walks at night.
Something's changed.
The stars don't shine

as bright. The trees just look
sterner. What happened?
Can't anyone take a joke?
These days the lights

in the houses turn off
earlier than they used to,
so that we're walking now
in almost pitch darkness.

And there are no high school kids
in their parents' cars,
rolling down their windows
and swearing at us.

Broken Ankle

For Hollie

1
And in that second inside of a second,
the truck rolling towards her, head-on—

she thought of something her mother
had once told her, how in accidents involving
drunk drivers, the drunk drivers often escape
unharmed—

2
Because their bodies are loose,
their minds aren't calculating
the impact.

3
And in that fraction of an infinitesimal fraction,
she somehow convinced her own body to do likewise—
to lean into the soul of death;

at 75 mph
to go somewhere else;

to play dead body
at the bottom of a swimming pool—

4
And didn't even brake.

Walk

Sometimes it catches
me by surprise
the sound of my own

footsteps down
an empty street at night

the scuffing sound
of my heels

so intimate and familiar

All alone with
nobody else to
hear it

Is that someone in the window

It reminds me that I'm
going somewhere

I'm pretty sure
that I am

One Night Only

My son, 13 years old, still plays
1-on-1 with me in the driveway,
on the seven-foot hoop

both of us can dunk on.
Now and then I wonder
how many games we have left—

young blood, old duffer—
Tonight I rebound one off the backboard,
pump fake, then go up strong,

like Coach taught me,
with everything I've got—
a good five, no six inches off the ground—

and he blocks me, the little punk.
Next thing I know he's throwing it down hard,
one-handed—right on my head.

And it goes on like that, blue evening—
into a new evening,
where for the first time in my life,

I don't mind so much
getting my ass whupped.

Epilogue

All those things we looked forward to
are behind us now, like mountain ranges,
with only the plain before us,

and a silver blue sea after that.
How many years did we travel to get here?
Love, it's getting hard to keep track.

Now that there's nothing
standing in our way, now that we
can finally see the horizon,

will we stay where we are
and write poems, or keep going
just a little bit further?

Dave Nielsen is the author of *Unfinished Figures*, winner of the 2016 Blue Lynx Prize for Poetry. His work has appeared in *The Southern Review, Southern Poetry Review, Tampa Review, South Carolina Review, 2River View, Aethlon,* and numerous other literary journals and magazines. He studied English at the University of Cincinnati and now lives in Salt Lake City with his wife and kids.

www.ingramcontent.com/pod-product-compliance
Lightning Source LLC
Jackson TN
JSHW022339030525
83713JS00003B/173